SCRIPTURE
JOURNAL

ENGLISH STANDARD VERSION

1–2 THESSALONIANS

CROSSWAY

WHEATON, ILLINOIS — ESV.ORG

RRDS	26	25	24	23	22	21	20	19	18	17
12	11	10	9	8	7	6	5	4	3	2	1

PREFACE

The Bible

The words of the Bible are the very words of God our Creator speaking to us. They are completely truthful;[1] they are pure;[2] they are powerful;[3] and they are wise and righteous.[4] We should read these words with reverence and awe,[5] and with joy and delight.[6] Through these words God gives us eternal life,[7] and daily nourishes our spiritual lives.[8]

The ESV Translation

The English Standard Version® (ESV®) stands in the classic stream of English Bible translations that goes back nearly five centuries. In this stream, accurate faithfulness to the original text is combined with simplicity, beauty, and dignity of expression. Our goal has been to carry forward this legacy for this generation and generations to come.

The ESV is an "essentially literal" translation that seeks as far as possible to reproduce the meaning and structure of the original text and the personal style of each Bible writer. We have sought to be "as literal as possible" while maintaining clear expression and literary excellence. Therefore the ESV is well suited for both personal reading and church ministry, for devotional reflection and serious study, and for Scripture memorization.

---

[1] Ps. 119:160; Prov. 30:5; Titus 1:2; Heb. 6:18 [2] Ps. 12:6 [3] Jer. 23:29; Heb. 4:12; 1 Pet. 1:23
[4] Ps. 19:7–11 [5] Deut. 28:58; Ps. 119:74; Isa. 66:2 [6] Ps. 19:7–11; 119:14, 97, 103; Jer. 15:16
[7] John 6:68; 1 Pet. 1:23 [8] Deut. 32:46; Matt. 4:4

The ESV Publishing Team

The ESV publishing team has included more than a hundred people. The fourteen-member Translation Oversight Committee benefited from the work of fifty biblical experts serving as Translation Review Scholars and from the comments of the more than fifty members of the Advisory Council. This international team from many denominations shares a common commitment to the truth of God's Word and to historic Christian orthodoxy.

To God's Honor and Praise

We know that no Bible translation is perfect; but we also know that God uses imperfect and inadequate things to his honor and praise. So to God the Father, Son, and Holy Spirit—and to his people—we offer what we have done, with our prayers that it may prove useful, with gratitude for much help given, and with ongoing wonder that our God should ever have entrusted to us so momentous a task.

To God alone be the glory!
The Translation Oversight Committee

1 THESSALONIANS

Greeting

1 Paul, Silvanus, and Timothy,

To the church of the Thessalonians in God the Father and the Lord Jesus Christ:

Grace to you and peace.

The Thessalonians' Faith and Example

² We give thanks to God always for all of you, constantly mentioning you in our prayers, ³ remembering before our God and Father your work of faith and labor of love and steadfastness of hope in our Lord Jesus Christ. ⁴ For we know, brothers loved by God, that he has chosen you, ⁵ because our gospel came to you not only in word, but also in power and in the Holy Spirit and with full conviction. You know what kind of men we proved to be among you for your sake. ⁶ And you became imitators of us and of the Lord, for you received the word in much affliction, with the joy of the Holy Spirit, ⁷ so that you became an example to all the believers in Macedonia and in Achaia. ⁸ For not only has the word of the Lord sounded forth from you in Macedonia and Achaia, but your faith in God has gone forth everywhere, so that we need not say anything. ⁹ For they themselves report concerning us the kind of reception we

had among you, and how you turned to God from idols to serve the living and true God, ¹⁰ and to wait for his Son from heaven, whom he raised from the dead, Jesus who delivers us from the wrath to come.

Paul's Ministry to the Thessalonians

2 For you yourselves know, brothers, that our coming to you was not in vain. ² But though we had already suffered and been shamefully treated at Philippi, as you know, we had boldness in our God to declare to you the gospel of God in the midst of much conflict. ³ For our appeal does not spring from error or impurity or any attempt to deceive, ⁴ but just as we have been approved by God to be entrusted with the gospel, so we speak, not to please man, but to please God who tests our hearts. ⁵ For we never came with words of flattery, as you know, nor with a pretext for greed—God is witness. ⁶ Nor did we seek glory from people, whether from you or from others, though we could have made demands as apostles of Christ. ⁷ But we were gentle among you, like a nursing mother taking care of her own children. ⁸ So, being affectionately desirous of you, we were ready to share with you not only the gospel of God but also our own selves, because you had become very dear to us.

⁹ For you remember, brothers, our labor and toil: we worked night and day, that we might not be a burden to any of you, while we proclaimed to you the gospel of God. ¹⁰ You are witnesses, and God also, how holy and righteous and blameless was our conduct toward you believers. ¹¹ For you know how, like a father with his children, ¹² we exhorted each one of you and encouraged you and charged you to walk in a manner worthy of God, who calls you into his own kingdom and glory.

¹³ And we also thank God constantly for this, that when you received the word of God, which you heard from us, you accepted it not as the word of men but as what it really is, the word of God, which is at work in you believers. ¹⁴ For you, brothers, became imitators of the churches of God in Christ Jesus that are in Judea. For you suffered the same things from your own countrymen as they did from the Jews, ¹⁵ who killed both the Lord Jesus and the prophets, and drove us out, and displease God and oppose all mankind ¹⁶ by hindering us from speaking to the Gentiles that they might be saved—so as always to fill up the measure of their sins. But wrath has come upon them at last!

Paul's Longing to See Them Again

¹⁷ But since we were torn away from you, brothers, for a short time, in person not in heart, we endeavored the more eagerly and with great desire to see you face to face, ¹⁸ because we wanted to come to you—I, Paul, again and again—but Satan hindered us. ¹⁹ For what is our hope or joy or crown of boasting before our Lord Jesus at his coming? Is it not you? ²⁰ For you are our glory and joy.

3 Therefore when we could bear it no longer, we were willing to be left behind at Athens alone, ² and we sent Timothy, our brother and God's coworker in the gospel of Christ, to establish and exhort you in your faith, ³ that no one be moved by these afflictions. For you yourselves know that we are destined for this. ⁴ For when we were with you, we kept telling you beforehand that we were to suffer affliction, just as it has come to pass, and just as you know. ⁵ For this reason, when I could bear it no longer, I sent to learn about your faith, for fear that

somehow the tempter had tempted you and our labor would be in vain.

Timothy's Encouraging Report

⁶ But now that Timothy has come to us from you, and has brought us the good news of your faith and love and reported that you always remember us kindly and long to see us, as we long to see you — ⁷ for this reason, brothers, in all our distress and affliction we have been comforted about you through your faith. ⁸ For now we live, if you are standing fast in the Lord. ⁹ For what thanksgiving can we return to God for you, for all the joy that we feel for your sake before our God, ¹⁰ as we pray most earnestly night and day that we may see you face to face and supply what is lacking in your faith?

¹¹ Now may our God and Father himself, and our Lord Jesus, direct our way to you, ¹² and may the Lord make you increase and abound in love for one another and for all, as we do for you, ¹³ so that he may establish your hearts blameless in holiness before our God and Father, at the coming of our Lord Jesus with all his saints.

A Life Pleasing to God

4 Finally, then, brothers, we ask and urge you in the Lord Jesus, that as you received from us how you ought to walk and to please God, just as you are doing, that you do so more and more. ² For you know what instructions we gave you through the Lord Jesus. ³ For this is the will of God, your sanctification: that you abstain from sexual immorality; ⁴ that each one of you know how to control his own body in holiness and honor, ⁵ not in the passion of lust like the Gentiles who do not

know God; [6] that no one transgress and wrong his brother in this matter, because the Lord is an avenger in all these things, as we told you beforehand and solemnly warned you. [7] For God has not called us for impurity, but in holiness. [8] Therefore whoever disregards this, disregards not man but God, who gives his Holy Spirit to you.

[9] Now concerning brotherly love you have no need for anyone to write to you, for you yourselves have been taught by God to love one another, [10] for that indeed is what you are doing to all the brothers throughout Macedonia. But we urge you, brothers, to do this more and more, [11] and to aspire to live quietly, and to mind your own affairs, and to work with your hands, as we instructed you, [12] so that you may walk properly before outsiders and be dependent on no one.

The Coming of the Lord

[13] But we do not want you to be uninformed, brothers, about those who are asleep, that you may not grieve as others do who have no hope. [14] For since we believe that Jesus died and rose again, even so, through Jesus, God will bring with him those who have fallen asleep. [15] For this we declare to you by a word from the Lord, that we who are alive, who are left until the coming of the Lord, will not precede those who have fallen asleep. [16] For the Lord himself will descend from heaven with a cry of command, with the voice of an archangel, and with the sound of the trumpet of God. And the dead in Christ will rise first. [17] Then we who are alive, who are left, will be caught up together with them in the clouds to meet the Lord in the air, and so we will always be with the Lord. [18] Therefore encourage one another with these words.

The Day of the Lord

5 Now concerning the times and the seasons, brothers, you have no need to have anything written to you. ²For you yourselves are fully aware that the day of the Lord will come like a thief in the night. ³While people are saying, "There is peace and security," then sudden destruction will come upon them as labor pains come upon a pregnant woman, and they will not escape. ⁴But you are not in darkness, brothers, for that day to surprise you like a thief. ⁵For you are all children of light, children of the day. We are not of the night or of the darkness. ⁶So then let us not sleep, as others do, but let us keep awake and be sober. ⁷For those who sleep, sleep at night, and those who get drunk, are drunk at night. ⁸But since we belong to the day, let us be sober, having put on the breastplate of faith and love, and for a helmet the hope of salvation. ⁹For God has not destined us for wrath, but to obtain salvation through our Lord Jesus Christ, ¹⁰who died for us so that whether we are awake or asleep we might live with him. ¹¹Therefore encourage one another and build one another up, just as you are doing.

Final Instructions and Benediction

¹²We ask you, brothers, to respect those who labor among you and are over you in the Lord and admonish you, ¹³and to esteem them very highly in love because of their work. Be at peace among yourselves. ¹⁴And we urge you, brothers, admonish the idle, encourage the fainthearted, help the weak, be patient with them all. ¹⁵See that no one repays anyone evil for evil, but always seek to do good to one another and to everyone. ¹⁶Rejoice always, ¹⁷pray without ceasing, ¹⁸give thanks in all circumstances; for this is the will of God in Christ Jesus for you.

[19] Do not quench the Spirit. [20] Do not despise prophecies, [21] but test everything; hold fast what is good. [22] Abstain from every form of evil.

[23] Now may the God of peace himself sanctify you completely, and may your whole spirit and soul and body be kept blameless at the coming of our Lord Jesus Christ. [24] He who calls you is faithful; he will surely do it.

[25] Brothers, pray for us.

[26] Greet all the brothers with a holy kiss.

[27] I put you under oath before the Lord to have this letter read to all the brothers.

[28] The grace of our Lord Jesus Christ be with you.

2 THESSALONIANS

Greeting

1 Paul, Silvanus, and Timothy,
To the church of the Thessalonians in God our Father and the Lord Jesus Christ:
² Grace to you and peace from God our Father and the Lord Jesus Christ.

Thanksgiving

³ We ought always to give thanks to God for you, brothers, as is right, because your faith is growing abundantly, and the love of every one of you for one another is increasing. ⁴ Therefore we ourselves boast about you in the churches of God for your steadfastness and faith in all your persecutions and in the afflictions that you are enduring.

The Judgment at Christ's Coming

⁵ This is evidence of the righteous judgment of God, that you may be considered worthy of the kingdom of God, for which you are also suffering— ⁶ since indeed God considers it just to repay with affliction those who afflict you, ⁷ and to grant relief to you who are afflicted as well as to us, when the Lord Jesus is revealed from heaven with his mighty angels ⁸ in

flaming fire, inflicting vengeance on those who do not know God and on those who do not obey the gospel of our Lord Jesus. [9] They will suffer the punishment of eternal destruction, away from the presence of the Lord and from the glory of his might, [10] when he comes on that day to be glorified in his saints, and to be marveled at among all who have believed, because our testimony to you was believed. [11] To this end we always pray for you, that our God may make you worthy of his calling and may fulfill every resolve for good and every work of faith by his power, [12] so that the name of our Lord Jesus may be glorified in you, and you in him, according to the grace of our God and the Lord Jesus Christ.

The Man of Lawlessness

2 Now concerning the coming of our Lord Jesus Christ and our being gathered together to him, we ask you, brothers, [2] not to be quickly shaken in mind or alarmed, either by a spirit or a spoken word, or a letter seeming to be from us, to the effect that the day of the Lord has come. [3] Let no one deceive you in any way. For that day will not come, unless the rebellion comes first, and the man of lawlessness is revealed, the son of destruction, [4] who opposes and exalts himself against every so-called god or object of worship, so that he takes his seat in the temple of God, proclaiming himself to be God. [5] Do you not remember that when I was still with you I told you these things? [6] And you know what is restraining him now so that he may be revealed in his time. [7] For the mystery of lawlessness is already at work. Only he who now restrains it will do so until he is out of the way. [8] And then the lawless one will be revealed, whom the Lord Jesus will kill with the breath of his mouth and bring to nothing

by the appearance of his coming. ⁹ The coming of the lawless one is by the activity of Satan with all power and false signs and wonders, ¹⁰ and with all wicked deception for those who are perishing, because they refused to love the truth and so be saved. ¹¹ Therefore God sends them a strong delusion, so that they may believe what is false, ¹² in order that all may be condemned who did not believe the truth but had pleasure in unrighteousness.

Stand Firm

¹³ But we ought always to give thanks to God for you, brothers beloved by the Lord, because God chose you as the firstfruits to be saved, through sanctification by the Spirit and belief in the truth. ¹⁴ To this he called you through our gospel, so that you may obtain the glory of our Lord Jesus Christ. ¹⁵ So then, brothers, stand firm and hold to the traditions that you were taught by us, either by our spoken word or by our letter.

¹⁶ Now may our Lord Jesus Christ himself, and God our Father, who loved us and gave us eternal comfort and good hope through grace, ¹⁷ comfort your hearts and establish them in every good work and word.

Pray for Us

3 Finally, brothers, pray for us, that the word of the Lord may speed ahead and be honored, as happened among you, ² and that we may be delivered from wicked and evil men. For not all have faith. ³ But the Lord is faithful. He will establish you and guard you against the evil one. ⁴ And we have confidence in the Lord about you, that you are doing and will do the things that we command. ⁵ May the Lord direct your hearts to the love of God and to the steadfastness of Christ.

Warning Against Idleness

⁶ Now we command you, brothers, in the name of our Lord Jesus Christ, that you keep away from any brother who is walking in idleness and not in accord with the tradition that you received from us. ⁷ For you yourselves know how you ought to imitate us, because we were not idle when we were with you, ⁸ nor did we eat anyone's bread without paying for it, but with toil and labor we worked night and day, that we might not be a burden to any of you. ⁹ It was not because we do not have that right, but to give you in ourselves an example to imitate. ¹⁰ For even when we were with you, we would give you this command: If anyone is not willing to work, let him not eat. ¹¹ For we hear that some among you walk in idleness, not busy at work, but busybodies. ¹² Now such persons we command and encourage in the Lord Jesus Christ to do their work quietly and to earn their own living.

¹³ As for you, brothers, do not grow weary in doing good. ¹⁴ If anyone does not obey what we say in this letter, take note of that person, and have nothing to do with him, that he may be ashamed. ¹⁵ Do not regard him as an enemy, but warn him as a brother.

Benediction

¹⁶ Now may the Lord of peace himself give you peace at all times in every way. The Lord be with you all.

¹⁷ I, Paul, write this greeting with my own hand. This is the sign of genuineness in every letter of mine; it is the way I write. ¹⁸ The grace of our Lord Jesus Christ be with you all.